DIESELS
IN THE
CAPITAL

Class 59 No. 59001 *Yeoman Endeavour* approaches West Drayton with the 10.05 (Saturdays) Acton Yard to Merehead empty hoppers, on 27th June 1987.

Class 50 No. 50020 *Revenge* leaves Kensington Olympia with empty stock for Willesden Carriage Sidings on a fine spring morning in 1984.

DIESELS
IN THE
CAPITAL

BRIAN BEER

Oxford Publishing Co.

A FOULIS-OPC Railway Book

British Library Cataloguing in Publication Data
Beer, Brian
  Diesels in the capital.
  1.   Southern England. Railway services: British Rail.
  Diesel locomotives, history
  I.   Title
  625.2'66'09422

ISBN 0 86093 418 7

Library of Congress catalog card number
89-85901

Published by:
Haynes Publishing Group
Sparkford, Near Yeovil, Somerset. BA22 7JJ

Haynes Publications Inc.
861 Lawrence Drive, Newbury Park, California 91320, USA.

Printed by J.H. Haynes & Co. Ltd

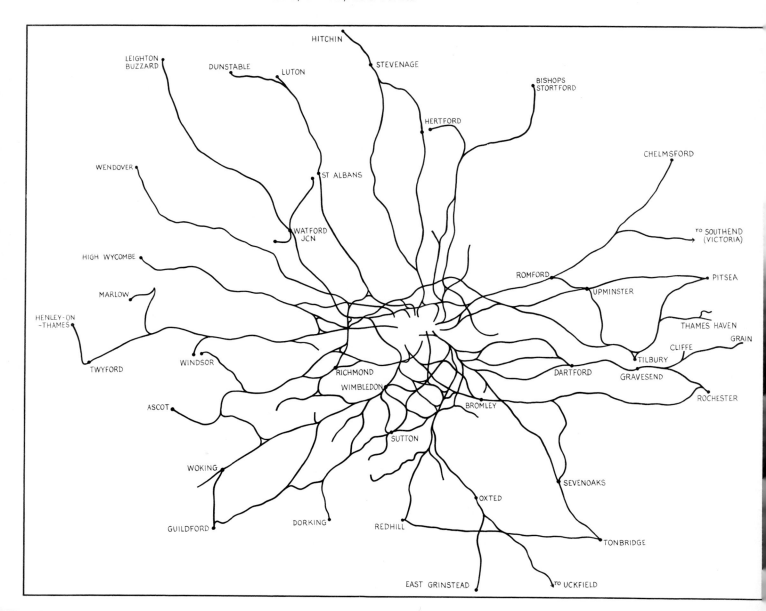

Introduction

To the casual observer, the railways of London may appear to lack the obvious appeal of other, well-documented, and frequently photographed routes. However, closer inspection reveals a variety of motive power, traffic, and railway history, to be found nowhere else in the country.

In spite of the inroads made by colour-light signalling, mechanical signal boxes of 14 different railway companies are still to be found in use, and all the main electrified routes still see diesel working on a regular basis. In addition, there are very few main line diesel locomotive classes which have not operated in the area at one time or another. It is this variety that *Diesels in the Capital* tries to reflect.

The area covered by this volume extends approximately 30 miles from the Central London termini in order to allow the inclusion of various lines of which photographs are rarely seen. Whilst the overall intention has been to illustrate London's railways in the 1980s, a number of views from earlier diesel days have been included, in an attempt to record some of the major changes which have taken place in the last 25 years. In selecting the material, I have tried to include new locations and viewpoints, as well as some of the better known positions, and have given coverage to the less successful classes of locomotive, as well as those which have been acclaimed by enthusiasts.

On a technical note, the majority of the photographs in the book have been taken with HP5 or XP1 film in a Mamiya 645 camera, and printed on Agfa resin-coated papers. Unless stated otherwise photographs were taken by the author. In conclusion, my thanks go to the large number of railwaymen, and other friends, who have assisted by providing information and other facilities, and particularly to Brian Morrison, whose invaluable advice and assistance have made this book possible.

Brian Beer
South London

Contents

Main Line Passenger Traffic

Class 50 No. 50040 *Leviathan* approaches Acton Main Line with the 14.10 Paddington to Oxford service, during February 1986. This locomotive was subsequently renamed *Centurion*, and withdrawn from service at the end of 1989.

The Great Western Main Line

Brush Traction prototype No. 1200 *Falcon* awaits departure from Paddington with a Bristol service in the early 1970s.

On Sunday 23rd August 1987, services normally using Marylebone were diverted to and from Paddington due to engineering work. A mixed formation dmu of Classes 108/115 leaves Paddington forming the 11.39 to High Wycombe.

Two generations of 'Warships' are depicted in these two photographs. North British A1A-A1A diesel hydraulic No. D603 *Conquest* (above) approaches West Ealing with the 11.05 Weston-super-Mare to Paddington on 25th July 1959, whilst Class 50 No. 50035 *Ark Royal* (below) crosses from "Main" to "Relief" lines at Longfield Junction, as it approaches the same location with the 11.00 Paddington to Oxford on 5th July 1987.

John Faulkner (above)

Although designated TOPS Class 35, the Beyer Peacock & Co. "Hymeks" did not survive to be re-numbered as such, the last representatives being withdrawn from Old Oak Common depot in March 1975. Here a member of the class heads the 13.00 Worcester to Paddington through Ealing Broadway in June 1972.

Class 50 No. 50005 *Collingwood* crosses the Grand Union Canal near Hayes and Harlington with the 09.45 Paddington to Plymouth working on 21st September 1986.

Class 52 'Western' No. 1013 *Western Ranger* speeds the 12.20 Penzance to Paddington express past Twyford on 7th October 1976, only a few months before this much-admired class was finally withdrawn from service. (This particular example survives today on the Severn Valley Railway.)

A down HST passes Twyford and heads into Sonning Cutting, and a freezing sunset, on 10th February 1985.

Via Greenford

Above: Class 47 No. 47620 passes Park Royal with the diverted 08.42 Paddington to Oxford service on 10th February 1985. Due to the renewal of a bridge in the Acton area, trains were being diverted via the Greenford Loop, rejoining the main line at Hanwell.

Right: Class 50 No. 50015 *Valiant* approaches South Ruislip at the head of the 17.40 Paddington to Wolverhampton, 31st July 1985. This train, and the corresponding up working, are the only surviving loco-hauled passenger trains to be routed via High Wycombe to Banbury.

Waterloo to Woking

Glimpsed through ornate ironwork incorporating the famous Waterloo lions, the 09.38 from Exeter rolls to a halt at its London destination, behind Class 50 No. 50047 *Swiftsure*.

Swindon-built 'Warship' No. D816 *Eclipse* passes Vauxhall with an Exeter to Waterloo working in July 1965. Motive power for these services was then, as now, provided by the Western Region, and *Eclipse* was part of the 84A (Laira) allocation.

Class 47/3 No. 47345 provides unusual motive power for the 11.10 Waterloo to Exeter on 14th July 1985, seen passing the site of the former Nine Elms steam shed on the right.

Temporarily re-formed four-car Class 204 unit No. 204004 passes Wimbledon forming the 12.10 Waterloo to Salisbury on 11th November 1987, only a few days before being withdrawn from service.

Although the 09.36 Exeter to Waterloo was diagrammed for a Class 33 locomotive on Saturdays in 1987, the use of sub-class 33/1 was unusual. No. 33114 is shown in Clapham Cutting on 8th August 1987.

Several ex-LSWR signal boxes remain in use between Waterloo and Woking. This example at New Malden controls the junction with the line to Shepperton and Twickenham. Class 50 No. 50029 *Renown* passes with the 12.20 Exeter to Waterloo on 11th June 1985.

Central Division

Above: Class 45/1 No. 45113 approaches Norbury with the 18.48 Brighton to Derby on 20th June 1985. This was one of several occasions during the year that a 'Peak' replaced the normal Class 47 on this inter-regional working.

Right: Class 201 unit No. 1002 passes Holmethorpe (north of Redhill) on a diverted Charing Cross to Hastings working in March 1982. The steeply-graded connection on the right leads to the British Industrial Sand sidings.

Above: Running down from Honor Oak Park towards Brockley, Class 33 No. 33053 heads the 08.25 East Grinstead to London Bridge commuter train in the morning mist of 12th September 1985.

Left: Class 207 (3D) unit No. 207010 leaves East Croydon with the 07.42 Uckfield to Victoria on 11th July 1987. With the electrification of the East Grinstead branch a few months later, through workings from Uckfield to London were reduced to a handful in peak hours only.

South Eastern Scenes

Above: Inter-regional services to and from Dover are usually the monopoly of Class 47s, but substitutions by other classes occasionally occur, as seen here. Class 33 No. 33013 leaves Bromley South with the 17.45 Dover Western Docks to Manchester service on 1st June 1986.

Right: Class 201 unit No. 1007 is at the head of the 11.43 from Hastings, as it passes New Cross on the final stage of its journey to Charing Cross, on 25th January 1986. Note the London Underground "D-stock" train arriving from Whitechapel in the background.

On the Great Eastern

Class 31 No. 31412 passes Bow Junction with empty stock from Bounds Green to Liverpool Street, to form a special "Ford Executive" working to Witham. The track in the extreme right foreground now forms part of the Stratford branch of the Docklands Light Railway, the other line giving access to the LT&S at Gas Factory Junction.

The Class 31s have been associated with the Great Eastern for some 30 years, since their introduction in 1957. In this view, Brush Type 2 No. D5522 (later 31418) is seen between duties at Liverpool Street in August 1969.

This side-view of Class 31 No. 31247 passing Stratford with an up boat train shows clearly the recess in the cab door where single line token equipment was carried.

Class 47 No. 47482 passes Chadwell Heath with the 10.30 Liverpool Street to Norwich on 4th April 1985. These workings were diagrammed for Class 86 electric locomotives from the following month.

On 16th February 1986, the overhead power supply was not available between Romford and Ilford because of engineering work. As a result, electric units were diesel-hauled over this stretch. Having just been attached to the train, Class 47 No. 47277 leaves Romford hauling Class 312 unit No. 312798 on an up working.

Many of the stations between Liverpool Street and Chelmsford retain Great Eastern character, typified by this seat, with GER lettering, seen at Ilford.

Having stood for 120 years, the North London Railway's terminus at Broad Street was demolished in 1985, and the site redeveloped. This view was taken on the first day of demolition, 29th June.

In happier days, a Class 125 dmu waits to depart as the 12.24 to Hatfield, alongside a Class 501 emu on a train to Richmond, 25th July 1970. The few remaining peak-hour workings were diverted via the Graham Road Curve into Liverpool Street when Broad Street finally closed. *John Faulkner*

Farewell
Broad Street

King's Cross Variety

Two generations of express motive power at King's Cross are shown in these views. In June 1965, 'Deltic' No. D9000 *Royal Scots Grey* leaves with the "Flying Scotsman", whilst No. D9013 *The Black Watch* waits to follow. The current equivalent is represented by HST power cars Nos 43051 *The Duke and Duchess of York* and 43179 at the rear of the 14.00 Edinburgh and 14.10 Leeds departures respectively, on 23rd August 1987.

"Baby Deltic" (Class 23) No. D5904 arrives at King's Cross with a morning commuter train in June 1965.

Type 1 Bo-Bo (Class 15) No. D8238 hauls empty stock up Holloway Bank in August 1962.

Brian Morrison

Commuting 1950s-style. North British Type 2 No. D6102 pauses at Aldersgate & Barbican on the 18.13 Moorgate to Welwyn Garden City working, on 10th June 1959.

John Faulkner

Commuting 1980s-style. Class 40 No. 40152 thunders past Hitchin on 27th July 1983, heading the 17.08 King's Cross to Peterborough.

The unsightly impact of electrification is very evident as Class 31 No. 31406 struggles past Harringay with a 15.05 departure to King's Lynn, which had started from King's Cross rather than Liverpool Street due to engineering work, on Sunday 22nd November 1987.

On 20th November 1986, HST power car No. 43194 *Royal Signals* heads a down express passing Marshmoor. The sleepers in the foreground had been recovered from a redundant siding previously used by Kelloggs.

Demolition of Somers Town goods yard (in the foreground) enabled this view of the superb train shed at St Pancras to be obtained in February 1986.

Midland Main Line

Many of the Birmingham Railway Carriage & Wagon Company Type 2 locomotives (later Classes 26 and 27) were allocated to the London area when new. Seen here on station pilot duties at St Pancras, No. D5392 (later 27120, then 27202) spent 16 months in the Capital before heading north, being finally withdrawn from Eastfield depot, Glasgow in 1980.

Class 37 locomotives were booked to work the 15.30 (Fridays only) Derby to St Pancras, plus the 18.20 return working, for a short period in 1988. No. 37429 *Eisteddfod Genedlaethol* is seen at the London terminus on 7th October, the first day of operation of the diagram.

A rare visitor to St Pancras on 2nd September 1982, was Class 56 No. 56002 which arrived on the 15.10 from Sheffield, and is seen awaiting departure with the 19.24 return working. Class 45 No. 45135 *3rd Carabinier* is in charge of empty stock, in the adjacent platform.

In this pre-electrification view at St Albans, a Class 45 heads a down express in April 1978, framed beneath a semaphore signal gantry.

A Leeds to St Pancras train passes Elstree in July 1959, hauled by a pair of the infamous Metropolitan-Vickers Co-Bos, Nos D5706 and D5700. The two Class 28 locomotives were at the time less than a year old, and were allocated to Derby shed (17A).

J.D. Croft

Although electrification came to Euston more than 20 years ago, diesel haulage beneath the wires still frequently occurs, either as an operating convenience, or due to a shortage of electric locomotives. On several Sundays in April 1984 engineering work led to diesel haulage of trains between Willesden and Euston. Class 31 No. 31213, (above), hauls Class 87 No. 87034 *William Shakespeare* and the 11.50 Euston to Manchester, seen north of Queen's Park on 1st April. One week later (below), Class 25 No. 25057 leads Class 86/3 No. 86312 *Elizabeth Garrett Anderson* on the 13.50 Willesden to Euston ecs, at the same location.

Euston to Watford

Certain HST power cars were modified during 1987 to enable them to be used in push-pull trials with electric locomotives. On 25th February 1988, No. 43123 was at the head of the 14.18 Birmingham to Euston as it passed Harrow and Wealdstone, with power being supplied from the rear by Class 86 No. 86240 *Bishop Eric Treacy*. The use of diesels under the wires in this way was a regular sight for some months.

Another regular diesel working under the wires is the empty stock of the Penzance to Paddington overnight train, seen here at West London Junction en route to Willesden for servicing. Class 50 No. 50035 *Ark Royal* provides motive power on 6th January 1985.

The nature of the environment in which early diesel locomotives had to survive can be seen clearly in this view of 1948-built Co-Co diesel electric No. 10001 at Willesden steam shed in October, 1964.

English Electric prototype DP2 arrives at Euston with a train from Liverpool, in pre-electrification days.

C.J. Marsden collection

Two Routes to the Chilterns

A Class 115 unit, led by DMBS No. M51896, passes the magnificent semaphore gantry at Neasden South Junction, and takes the High Wycombe line with the 16.52 Marylebone to Aylesbury working on 6th August 1987. The other route is used by trains to Aylesbury via Amersham.

A Class 115 unit passes West Ruislip, bound for Marylebone with a working from High Wycombe on 31st July 1985. Note the lower quadrant signals still in use here on former Great Western and Great Central Joint metals.

On the other route served by trains from Marylebone, Derby Class 115 DMBS No. M51663 leads an Aylesbury-bound working, approaching Wendover, on 15th November 1986.

Branch Line Traffic

Class 37 No. 37111, complete with snowploughs, shunts a permanent way train, amidst discarded fruit and vegetable packings at Stratford Market, on a fine June morning in 1984, and is well off the beaten track for an Eastfield-based machine.

A Class 105 Cravens unit on a North Woolwich to Camden Road working comes under semaphore signals as it passes Stratford Market in May 1984.

Another Cravens unit heads north between Custom House and Canning Town, in a bleak docklands landscape, on 9th January 1985, with signs of forthcoming electrification evident.

Stratford to North Woolwich

Several sources of freight traffic still remain on the North Woolwich branch, reminders of the once-numerous yards and sidings in the area. On the last surviving section of the Silvertown Tramway, Class 31 No. 31225 collects scrap metal, which it will trip to Temple Mills Yard, on 24th September 1985.

Another location receiving a daily trip working from Temple Mills is the Steetley chemical works at West Ham. Having collected the afternoon empty tanks, Class 08 No. 08810 attaches the brake van, ready for the leisurely return trip.

On the Banks of the Thames

Class 73 locomotives Nos 73121 *Croydon 1883-1983* and 73140 leave Angerstein Wharf with the 14.00 hours return empty hoppers to Cliffe on 11th January 1986. As this branch is not electrified, the train will be diesel powered at least until joining the main line at Angerstein Junction (Charlton).

One of the least photogenic lines in the London area, and possibly in the country, is that from Stanford-le-Hope to Thames Haven. In surroundings typical of the branch, Class 47 No. 47114 returns tanks from the terminus to Ripple Lane on 17th December 1986.

Traffic to the oil refineries at Grain, at the end of the branch from Hoo Junction, had fallen in recent years, reaching a level of only two or three trains a week at one stage. However, materials for the Channel Tunnel have now brought a new lease of life. In connection with aggregates traffic, Class 59 No. 59005 *Kenneth J Painter* undertook trial runs on the branch in 1989, and is seen here passing High Halstow with a special train from Grain to Hither Green, on 16th September.

A flash photograph of Grain Crossing box during the Siberian weather of January 1987.

Stratford was the last depot in the London area to retain an allocation of Class 03s, using them for shunting on the sharp curves at Poplar Docks. No. 03168 is seen dealing with steel traffic in June 1981, shortly before closure of the branch.

The RCTS "East London No.5" railtour passes the site of South Bromley station as it proceeds cautiously towards Poplar Docks, on 6th June 1981. An interesting combination of vehicles of Classes 105, 104 and 116 make up the seven-car formation. The trackbed seen here now forms part of the Docklands Light Railway.

On the last day of diesel operation, the green-liveried Class 105 unit, formed of Nos E53359 and E54122, approaches Emerson Park Halt, bound for Romford, on 10th May 1986. The single-line token for the branch was photographed on the same day.

Great Eastern Outposts

A Class 116 unit arrives at Southminster from Wickford on 4th April 1985. The GER signal box was abolished the following year. The overhead gantry used to lift nuclear flasks from rail to road transport can be seen on the extreme right.

Class 31 No. 31250 approaches Ware with 7E83, the 08.22 Willesden to Bishops Stortford (via Hertford East) working on 16th September 1987.

Luton to Dunstable

Above: Passing a lattice-post fixed distant signal, two Class 115 four-car units leave Dunstable, forming the "Chiltern Chariot II" railtour on 21st February 1987.

Right: A similar signal features in this view of Class 31 "Skinhead" No. 31138 approaching Luton (Bute St.) with the daily working of 6O93, the 18.45 Dunstable to Northfleet prior to the loss of the cement traffic on the branch. A pair of Class 33 locomotives will take the train forward from Luton to its destination in Kent.

The Hertford Loop

An up ballast train passes Cuffley in January 1972, behind a Class 31 locomotive.

May 1988 saw the withdrawal of sleeping cars from the East Coast Main Line. Shortly before the end, Class 47 No. 47662 was photographed passing Watton-at-Stone with the diverted 20.25 Aberdeen to King's Cross, conveying both Nightrider and sleeping accommodation, on 10th April 1988.

The peak hour only services on the short branch from Watford Junction to Croxley Green have generally been worked by electric units in recent years, of Classes 501 and, latterly, 313. During 1987, a shortage of serviceable emus led to occasional substitutions by Class 122 diesel single-cars, as on 3rd July, when No. 55011 paused briefly at Croxley Green before returning to the junction.

Change
at Watford Junction

A Class 108 unit (cars M51909 and M54271) pauses at Bricket Wood on a Watford Junction to St Albans Abbey working, 28th June 1987. Electrification of this branch commenced four months later.

Great Western Byways

The weekly oil train is shunted at Staines West by Class 47 No. 47009, prior to returning as 7E29, the 13.40 to Ripple Lane, on 14th September 1987.

Over thirty years before, GWR railcar No. W27W arrives at Staines West on the 2.10pm from West Drayton, on 10th April 1954. Passenger services ceased in 1965.

John Faulkner

Class 47 No. 47069 (now 47845) approaches Southall with the 08.50 (Sundays) Brentford to Appleford rubbish train, on 31st March 1985. The dmu depot in the background has since been closed as a diesel depot and is used for London's steam locomotive operations.

Unusual motive power for the empty "Binliner" returning from Appleford to Brentford on 2nd August 1987. Class 50 No. 50027 *Lion* deputises for the rostered Class 56 as it passes Southall and heads for the former GLC rubbish terminal.

Two Class 121 single-car units, Nos W55027 and W55022 are seen against a backdrop of Windsor Castle, as they pass Eton on a Slough to Windsor working, 20th June 1987.

Class 117 unit No. L413 leaves Wargrave on the 15.44 Henley to Twyford working on 14th September 1987.

In addition to the regular passenger service between Paddington and Greenford, worked by Class 121 single-car units, the Greenford Loop is a useful diversionary route when the main line is blocked between Hanwell and Old Oak West Junction. One such occasion was 25th November 1984, when Class 50 No. 50031 *Hood* on the 11.00 Oxford to Paddington approached South Greenford, and was viewed from the vandalised waiting-room.

Left: More severe weather condition prevailed on 10th February 1985, whe main line services again used the Green ford Loop. Class 50 No. 50035 *Ark Roy* at the head of the 10.55 Paddington Oxford passes Castle Bar Park.

Below: Traffic from the Guinness facto at Park Royal increased in July 198! when a £1.5 million contract was secure by Railfreight. Class 50 No. 5004 *Dauntless* is seen on the short branch from the factory, with more supplies fe the nation's public houses in two VGA on 30th August 1985.

Southern Rural Routes

Above: Class 33 No. 33052 *Ashford* passes Lingfield with ecs from East Grinstead to New Cross Gate, on the evening of 23rd July 1985, having previously worked the 17.50 London Bridge to East Grinstead commuter train.

Left: Another Class 33, No. 33017 works a return Pullman special from Lingfield to Victoria between Woldingham and Upper Warlingham on 28th June 1985.

Above: The Edenbridge lattice-post distant signal stands in the clear position as a three-car Class 119 unit approaches the station on a working from Redhill to Tonbridge, on 27th March 1986.

Opposite: On the same fine spring day, Class 207 unit No. 1301 is seen about to enter Edenbridge Tunnel and pass beneath the Redhill to Tonbridge line, on a Victoria to Uckfield train.

Above: Uckfield still retains facilities for loco-hauled trains, and receives occasional visits from these, although all regular trains are now demus. One notable occasion was 27th December 1986, when a railtour brought Class 45/1 No. 45104 *The Royal Warwickshire Fusiliers* to the terminus.

Left: The milepost in the foreground confirms that Class 33 No. 33045 is approximately one mile south of Hurst Green, as it heads for Eridge with a special train from Victoria conveying cyclists and their machines, prior to a two-wheeled tour of Sussex, on 12th October 1985.

Left: Class 207 unit No. 207023 approaches Birchden Junction (north of Eridge) with a Victoria to Uckfield train.

Below: Class 201 unit No. 1004 takes the cross-country route to Tonbridge, at Redhill, with a diverted Charing Cross to Hastings train in March 1982. The signals were removed under the final phase of the Brighton Line re-signalling scheme in 1985.

The Orbital Routes

Class 47 No. 47055 approaches Kensington Olympia under lower quadrant signals with a Norwood to Acton freight on 8th April 1981. The Olympia branch of the London Underground District Line can be seen on the right.

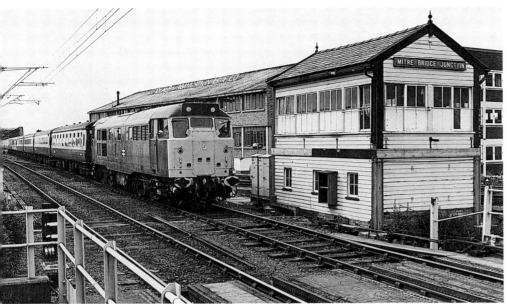

The West London Line

Class 31 No. 31468 passes Mitre Bridge Junction with empty stock from Paddington bound for Willesden on 29th June 1986.

Mitre Bridge Junction (Willesden) is the changeover point from electric to diesel traction for passenger trains bound for the Southern Region. The travellers on this "Mystex" from Blackpool on 20th April 1985, are probably unaware that their destination is to be Portsmouth, as Class 86 No. 86261 *Driver John Axon G.C.* leaves train 1Z37, to be replaced by Class 33 No. 33015 for the remainder of the journey. The Class 08 on the left has been used to transport the shunter to the scene!

Crossing the Grand Union Canal, just south of Mitre Bridge Junction, Class 33 No. 33052 *Ashford* heads for Willesden where it will be replaced by an electric locomotive, with a Sheerness to Mossend air-braked service, on 12th September 1985.

Later the same day, Class 33/2 No. 33202 is silhouetted against the setting sun at the same location, as it struggles towards Willesden with 6M94, a Dover to Bescot air-braked service.

Until 1981, Kensington Olympia was used as a Motorail terminus, and saw regular appearances of Class 50 locomotives, as in the view (above) of No. 50010 *Monarch* storming past White City with the 07.45 departure to St Austell on 13th July 1980. A mid-day departure was used for the service to Scotland, seen (right) leaving Olympia behind Class 25 locomotives Nos 25243 and 25054 on 31st May 1981

Class 33/1 No. 33109 awaits departure from Kensington Olympia with an evening service to Clapham Junction in June 1984, in the shadow of the former LNWR signal box at the south end of the station.

Class 73 No. 73105 heads for the Southern Region with a train of hoppers during December 1981 as it passes Kensington Olympia. This fine signal gantry has since been removed, but a mixture of upper and lower quadrant signals still remain.

With the Earls Court exhibition centre forming the backdrop, Class 47 No. 47401 *North Eastern* passes Lillie Bridge with the 12.15 Brighton to Liverpool on 12th January 1987.

Another Class 47 crosses the River Thames at Battersea Reach, at the head of the 09.58 Manchester to Brighton, 27th December 1985.

Leaving the Southern Region at Old Kew Junction, Class 47 No. 47093 proceeds cautiously towards Kew East Junction, and London Midland Region metals, in charge of a Southampton to Ripple Lane (Barking) Freightliner, on 20th August 1986.

In the sub-zero weather conditions of 7th February 1986, the 6O64 Ripple Lane to Micheldever tanks is headed by Class 47 No. 47313, taking the line to Old Kew Junction at Kew East Junction. The lines to the right lead to Clapham Junction, via New Kew Junction.

The line from Kew East Junction joins the electrified North London Link at South Acton. Class 50 No. 50024 *Vanguard* was a rare visitor on 25th November 1984, with ecs from Paddington to Willesden (routed via the Greenford Loop, Kensington Olympia, Clapham Junction and New Kew Junction). The lines to the left are used solely by passenger trains to Richmond.

Kensal Green Junction before rationalisation. In May 1984, two Class 56 locomotives with No. 56049 leading head for Acton Yard, with aggregate empties from Purfleet.

The junction layout at Kensal Green was completely re-modelled in April 1985. Two Class 31s, Nos 31260 and 31162 are seen in attendance.

Using the revised layout after completion, Class 37 No. 37001 heads for Ripple Lane with oil tanks on 20th April 1985. This locomotive has since been refurbished, and re-numbered 37707.

Climbing up from the West Coast Main Line towards Kensal Green Junction, a Liverpool to Highbury & Islington football excursion is in the care of Class 37 No. 37050, which has just taken over from a Class 85 electric locomotive, on 6th October 1984.

This unusual combination of motive power resulted from overhead line work in the Primrose Hill area, which caused the 13.30 (Sundays) Harwich Parkeston Quay to Birmingham to be diverted via Hampstead Heath. Class 37 No. 37057 drags Class 86 No. 86221 *BBC Look East* on the approach to Kensal Green Junction, on 23rd August 1987.

The North London Line crosses the main lines from King's Cross just east of Camden Road, and the southern portals of Copenhagen Tunnel are visible beneath Class 47 No. 47450 as it hauls Class 86 No. 86221 *BBC Look East* and the 07.50 Harwich Parkeston Quay to Glasgow and Edinburgh, towards Camden Road, on 15th August 1987.

A Class 105 unit (comprising Nos E53362 and E54420) climbs towards Highbury & Islington with a service from North Woolwich on 2nd April 1985.

On several occasions during 1985, services from Liverpool Street to Cambridge were diverted due to engineering work, and ran from Stratford via the North London Line, Canonbury Junction and the East Coast Main Line, reaching their destination via Royston. Two such workings are illustrated here, both powered by Class 31 locomotives rather than the diagrammed Class 47. The 10.35 Liverpool Street to Cambridge (above) passes Western Junction (Dalston) with No. 31181 in charge on 15th September, whilst (right) No. 31424 is at the head of 1C75, the 15.13 from King's Lynn to Liverpool Street, passing Dalston Kingsland on 8th September.

In addition to the 20-minute interval passenger service, the North London Line sees a regular flow of freight traffic. Class 59 No. 59002 *Yeoman Enterprise* passes Homerton with 6V29, Purfleet to Merehead hoppers, on 15th August 1986.

Class 50 No. 50042 *Triumph* passes Victoria Park Junction with a short freight returning from Temple Mills Yard (Stratford) to Acton Yard, on 4th May 1984. The line to Poplar Docks formerly diverged to the right of the signal box.   *Ken Brunt*

The freight-only line from Acton Wells Junction to Cricklewood is used by traffic from the Southern and Western Regions to gain access to the main lines from Euston (via Acton Canal Wharf), Marylebone (via Neasden Junction) and St Pancras (via Dudding Hill Junction). Passing the charming Midland Railway signal box, Class 50 No. 50004 *St Vincent* takes the single line to Willesden at Acton Canal Wharf with ecs from Paddington, on a fine June morning in 1984.

Acton Wells to Cricklewood

Dudding Hill Junction (Cricklewood) is also controlled by a Midland Railway structure, albeit of a later design, which gives access to the Midland Main Line in either a northbound or southbound direction. Class 45 No. 45110 (unofficially named *Medusa*) has come from the south with ecs from Bounds Green to Marylebone, to form a steam special, on 15th August 1987.

Gospel Oak
to Barking

A Class 104 unit on a Barking to Gospel Oak working passes Junction Road Junction. The famous Midland Railway signal box was closed in November 1985.

Approaching Upper Holloway, Class 47 No. 47380 heads for Ripple Lane (Barking) with eleven oil tank wagons in tow, on 24th April 1985.

Some HST sets used on services from St Pancras are maintained at Bounds Green depot, on the East Coast Main Line. An ecs working returning to St Pancras to form a Sunday morning departure drops down from Harringay and passes Harringay Park Junction, on 5th May 1985.

Forming part of the half-hourly interval passenger service between Gospel Oak and Barking, a Class 104 unit, led by DMBS No. M53453 of Cricklewood depot, rolls into Leytonstone High Road in April 1985.

Class 47 No. 47112 passes Woodgrange Park on 6M37, the 12.45 Dagenham Dock to Garston freight on 15th October 1987.

Opposite: Hastings-gauge Class 33 No. 33204 takes the Lewisham route at Nunhead Junction with a freight bound for Crayford on 28th June 1986.

Right: Taking the other route at Nunhead Junction, and far from its home depot of Gateshead, Class 47 No. 47404 *Hadrian* is in charge of the 09.03 Wolverhampton to Dover train, running via the Catford Loop Line because of engineering work, on Sunday 28th September 1986.

South Eastern

Sightings

Another loco-hauled working on the Catford Loop occurred when train 6M19, the 09.23 from Bat & Ball (Sevenoaks) to Mountsorrel, was diverted via this route on Saturday, 20th September 1986. Class 56 No. 56054 provided motive power, and is seen north of Crofton Park.

Approaching Bromley South en rou[te] from Watford to Dover and Ramsgat[e] Class 50s Nos 50026 *Indomitable* an[d] 50032 *Courageous* head "The Malt an[d] Hops" railtour on 29th October 1988.

Class 37 No. 37001 was a rare visitor t[o] the North Kent Line on 27th Octobe[r] 1986, when it was captured on fil[m] passing Plumstead with the diverte[d] Brookgate to Ripple Lane tanks.

Ken Brun[t]

No. D46 (later Class 45 No. 45037) required assistance from two brake tenders to control its train of coal empties, when photographed approaching Shortlands in the up direction on 23rd June 1970, at which time the 'Peak' was allocated to D16 (Nottingham Division).

Although the motive power and wagons have changed since 1970, through working to the Southern Region by London Midland locomotives and crews continues. Class 58 No. 58040 *Cottam Power Station* approaches Hither Green as it heads for its Northfleet destination with loaded coal hoppers from Toton on 23rd June 1988.

Left: In an urban landscape dominated by the dome of St Paul's Cathedral Class 33 No. 33055 crosses Blackfriars Junction with a Sunday engineers' train from Hither Green destined for Blackfriars, on 6th September 1987.

Right: During the adverse weather conditions which gripped the South East in January 1987, several Class 56 locomotives were used to haul electric units, in order to maintain services. No. 56001 is seen leaving Lewisham with two Class 411 units in tow on 15th January.

Below, right: A few hardy photographers braved the sub-zero conditions to record the scenes on the Southern Region in January, 1987. Snow-encrusted Class 56 No. 56062 is seen awaiting departure from Victoria for the Kent coast, with electric multiple units in tow.

Nick Ralph

Below: Loco-hauled workings are few and far between on the Mid-Kent line and a trip from Hayes to Bournemouth and return on 2nd May 1988, aroused much local interest. The return working of the chartered VSOE stock is seen here south of Catford Bridge powered by Class 33 No. 33029.

Some Central Lines

Class 47 locomotives are sometimes diagrammed for Southern Region internal services, one example being the 6Y64 Tolworth to Newhaven aggregate empties, seen here re-starting from Norwood Junction, after a crew change, in October 1987. Although booked for a Western Region Class 47/3, Crewe-allocated No. 47335 was in charge of the rake of PHAs. Note the condemned units of Classes 205 and 415/1 on the right.

Class 59 locomotives broke new ground from March 1988, when they began to appear on workings to Crawley New Yard. In this view, No. 59003 *Yeoman Highlander* passes South Croydon in June of that year, with train 6V29, the 09.43 return working from Crawley to Merehead. A Class 319 unit heads south on a Bedford to Brighton working.

The oil terminal at Selsdon is situated on the truncated remains of the Woodside to Sanderstead branch, which closed to passenger traffic in May 1983. In this view, Class 37 No. 37893 prepares to return to Ripple Lane with the empties (7L53), on 14th December 1988.

Local passengers look on as Class 33 No. 33027 *Earl Mountbatten of Burma* accelerates a Tattenham Corner to Manchester return Derby day charter through Tadworth, in June 1987.

A quiet Sunday morning scene at London Bridge, as the guard prepares for the departure of Class 33 No. 33026, with empty vans for New Cross Gate, on 25th October 1987.

Class 37 locomotives commenced operations between Didcot and Hove conveying coal traffic in January 1989. Passing East Croydon on 7th February, No. 37235 *The Coal Merchants' Association of Scotland* heads 6V04, the 12.05 return working from the south coast.

South Western Workings

Above: Class 37 No. 37239 pauses at Chessington South, prior to returning to Didcot with 6V32 coal empties, on 30th July 1987. A Class 455/8 emu waits in the other platform to return to Waterloo. Coal traffic to this location ceased in December 1988.

Right: Two former BR Class 04 0-6-0 shunters survive on the Chessington branch in industrial use. The former No. D2310 (now named *Colmec*) and No. D2246 are seen here at Tolworth Coal Concentration Depot during July 1987.

Left: Class 47 No. 47411 passes Barnes with ecs for Clapham Yard, off a Bradford to Twickenham charter, on 11th April 1987. This locomotive was named *The Geordie* a few weeks later, as a result of the withdrawal of No. 47403, which originally bore this name.

Centre, right: Dropping down from Clapham Junction, Class 56 No. 56013 passes beneath the Central Division main line from Victoria to Clapham Junction, as it approaches Culvert Road Junction with the 13.23 Toton to Northfleet loaded coal hoppers (7O85) on 30th July 1987.

Left: Windsor & Eton Riverside station retains facilities to receive loco-hauled trains, and is a popular destination for day trips. On 20th June 1987, Class 33 No. 33022 took charge of 1Z27, a Bolton to Windsor charter at Mitre Bridge Junction (Willesden), and is seen here passing Datchet with ecs to Clapham Yard after depositing the Lancastrian visitors at their destination.

Class 56 No. 56062 approaches Putney with hoppers from Bat & Ball to Mountsorrel on a fine Saturday morning in August 1986.

Class 50 No. 50039 *Implacable* approaches Sunningdale, having been diverted via Reading and Wokingham, with the 09.38 Exeter to Waterloo of 4th January 1986.

Special Traffic

A charter from High Wycombe, bound for a day on the coast at Bournemouth, gets a clear road through West Ruislip headed by Class 47 No. 47466 on 27th June 1987.

Day Trippers

On 8th June 1985, Class 50 No. 50035 *Ark Royal* worked throughout from Penzance to Wembley Central on a charter train. It is seen here on the return working, leaving the West Coast Main Line at Willesden, to travel via Acton Canal Wharf and Acton Wells Junction to gain the Western Region at Acton Main Line.

A football match at Southend generated sufficient away support to justify the running of a special through train from Manchester (Piccadilly) on 23rd September 1986. Class 47 No. 47108 heads 1Z25 at Dagenham East, overhauling a London Underground D-stock train on a District Line working from Ealing Broadway to Upminster. The "Footex" terminated at Westcliff.

Railtours

The "Class 46 Tribute" of 17th June 1984, was hauled by No. 46026 *Leicestershire and Derbyshire Yeomanry* seen here passing Upper Holloway on the Weymouth to Liverpool Street leg of the tour.

"The Bakers Dozen" tour of 28th June 1987, saw Class 45 No. 45062 leave Euston, only to fail near Kenton, Class 31 No. 31305 assisted, the unlikely duo being seen here north of Kenton.

Class 40 No. 40122 hauls *ETHEL 3* and the ''Pennine Forty Farewell'' railtour as it approaches Queen's Park on the climb out of Euston on 12th March 1988. The locomotive was in grey undercoat on this day, but was to appear in immaculate green livery a few weeks later on its last trip in BR ownership.

One of the few tours in the London area to use three locomotives simultaneously was ''Three to the Sea'', on 2nd May 1987, seen passing Lillie Bridge behind Class 20s Nos 20064, 20030 and 20118. This location is a favourite vantage point for photographers on the West London Line, offering a view of the London Underground depot (on the right) where an assortment of battery locomotives replenish their resources prior to nocturnal activities.

Pullman Travel

June 30th 1987, witnessed the rare sight of a loco-hauled departure from Blackfriars, when the Daily Mail newspaper chartered a Pullman special to Lingfield. Class 33 No. 33057 (complete with snowploughs!) was the rostered power, and is seen leaving the London terminus at 19.20 hours for the evening round trip.

An eight-car Blue Pullman on an up working approaches Twyford on 4th May 1973, shortly before these units were withdrawn from service.

The stock of the "Venice Simplon Orient Express" (VSOE) is maintained at Stewarts Lane depot (Battersea), and most trips from London originate from Victoria, regardless of destination. Class 33 No. 33015 passes beneath the Waterloo to Clapham Junction main line as it leaves Stewarts Lane with ecs for Victoria, to form a charter to Brighton on 21st November 1987.

Green-liveried Class 33 No. 33008 *Eastleigh* makes a fine sight with the VSOE stock in tow as it proceeds along the North London Line at rooftop level, with the Victoria to Norwich leg of an up-market railtour, approaching Homerton on 11th April 1987.

Track Recording

High-speed track-recording coach No. DB999550 was sandwiched between two Class 201 power cars (Nos 60009 and 60008) when passing Little Missenden on 25th April 1986. The train was en route from Aylesbury to cover parts of the London Underground Metropolitan Line.

The high-speed track-recording train heads for Fenchurch Street, above the arches west of Gas Factory Junction, on 14th September 1987, prior to working over both routes to Shoeburyness. Stratford's Class 47 No. 47579 *James Nightal G.C.* provides motive power on this occasion.

Test Coach *Iris* (No. RDB 975010) is a "Derby Lightweight" single car, originally numbered M79900, which saw service on the Banbury (Merton St.) branch in its younger days. It is now used by the Derby Research Centre for radio tests, and is seen here approaching Blackfriars on 26th March 1987.

Also based at Derby is this two-car Park Royal (Class 103) track-recording unit, known as "Laboratory 5", and dating from 1957. It has been used on the London Underground system on several occasions in recent years. Nos RDB 975090 and RDB 975089 prepare to leave Hammersmith (Metropolitan Line) station on 5th December 1984, running as 2Z24.

Main Line Freight Traffic

One of only a handful of freight trains still traversing the former Great Western and Great Central Joint Line is the daily working from Ripple Lane to Thame. The return working is seen here passing Gerrards Cross, behind Class 47 No. 47008, on 3rd July 1987. The through roads have been taken out of commission, forcing the train to use the platform loop.

Paddington to High Wycombe

Above: Class 47 No. 47344 heads the 6O58 Greenford to Halling cement train past North Acton, overtaking a London Underground Central Line train on the 12.07 Ealing Broadway to Loughton trip on 1st August 1987.

Right: Class 50 No. 50048 *Dauntless* is overtaken by an eastbound Central Line train as it arrives at Park Royal to collect traffic from the Guinness factory, in August 1985. The air-braked service is the 14.37 Reading to Willesden, which was diagrammed for a "Hoover" at this time.

Traffic at Acton Yard warranted the provision of two Class 08 shunting locomotives on 24th April 1984, as Class 25 No. 25234 propelled a freight train into position after arrival.

In sharp contrast with the scene opposite, ...cton Yard presents a sorry sight as Class ...9 No. 59001 *Yeoman Endeavour* departs ...ith empty hoppers to Merehead on 25th ...uly 1987.

Class 37 No. 37146 rattles along at Ruscombe, bound for Didcot with empty coal hoppers from Chessington, on 14th September 1987.

Above: The 09.00 Oxford to Old Oak Common vans (3A88) approach West Ealing on Sunday, 23rd August 1987, behind a pair of consecutively numbered Class 50 locomotives in Network SouthEast livery. Although rostered for two locomotives, this train was often hauled by only one, and No. 50018 *Resolution* plus No. 50019 *Ramillies* were a welcome sight for the photographer. This working ceased in July 1988 with the loss of newspaper traffic.

Right: Another train of empty vans arrives at Old Oak Common, picked out by the low evening sunlight, with Class 47 No.47314 in charge, on 14th April 1985.

Right: Class 128 single-car parcels unit No. W55992 leads a three-car Class 117 unit on the 19.22 Reading to Paddington service, past Old Oak Common depot on 3rd August 1985.

On the L.T and S.

Above: Class 56 locomotives Nos 56037 *Richard Trevithick* and 56031 *Merehead* thunder through Dagenham Dock with a Purfleet to Westbury stone train, during April 1985. This working has since been taken over by a single Class 59 locomotive.

Right: The nameplate of Stratford's pride and joy, Class 47 No. 47007, photographed at Ripple Lane in December 1987.

Above: The only regular loco-hauled train over the line via Laindon in 1986 was the thrice-weekly trip serving the military establishment at Shoeburyness. On 5th December, Class 37 No. 37109 performed the duty, and is seen approaching Dagenham East on the outward trip from Temple Mills. The London Underground District Line can be seen on the right.

Left: Class 37/7 No. 37893 (formerly 37237) departs from Ripple Lane West with an eastbound tank train on 31st December 1987.

Willesden to Bletchley

Above: Class 127 two-car diesel parcels unit No. 918 passes Kenton on an up working in June 1986.

Left: 1 Co-Co 1 diesel electric No. 10203 passes Headstone Lane with a down fitted freight on 22nd July 1961, before the advent of overhead electrification.

John Faulkner

Below: Diesel working under the wires on a regular basis continues, even after twenty years of electric operation. One such working is the daily King's Cross to Tring cement empties, seen here approaching Linslade Tunnel behind Class 31 locomotives Nos 31203 and 31180 on 18th September 1987.

Lines from Liverpool Street

Above: The majority of the through freight traffic over the main line from Stratford to Chelmsford consists of Freightliner trains to and from the Felixstowe terminals. Certain of these are hauled by pairs of Class 37 locomotives, one of which is 4E75, the 07.26 Garston to Felixstowe South, seen here passing Goodmayes behind Nos 37238 and 37091 on 21st November 1987.

Left: Class 31 No. 31414 approaches Wickford with a parcels train from Southend Victoria to Reading on 27th July 1987.

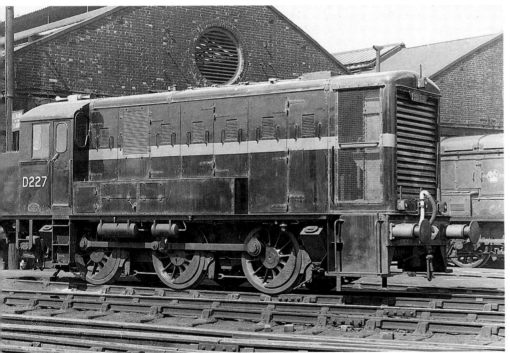

Above: Class 59 locomotives commenced operation between Acton Yard and Harlow Mill in 1987, although not on a daily basis. No. 59002 *Yeoman Enterprise* waits for the last PTAs to be unloaded before returning as 6V62, via Acton, to Merehead, on 16th September 1987.

Left: No. D227 an 0-6-0 diesel hydraulic shunter stands outside Stratford shed in June 1959, a few months before withdrawal. This prototype spent all of its brief career on loan to British Railways from the manufacturers (English Electric) and was re-numbered D0277 in August 1959, to avoid confusion with English Electric Type 4 (later Class 40) No. D227 which entered service at that time.

F.T. Hornby

Below: A load of YCVs passes Ilford on the up main line, in the hands of Class 47 No. 47310, in October 1987. The train has just passed beneath the flyover which was brought into use in 1947 to carry the ''electric lines'' over the ''main lines''.

From King's Cross
to Hitchin

Brush Type 2 No. 5545 (later No. 31127) approaches Finsbury Park in January 1972, with an up loaded ballast train. No. 5 signal box was one of seven mechanical installations which existed at this location before the advent of colour light signalling.

Class 37 No. 37077 emerges from Welwyn South Tunnel on 22nd March 1982, heading sand empties returning to Fen Drayton from King's Cross Yard. This working is one of the few to have brought these locomotives to the southern end of the East Coast Main Line on a regular basis.

Brian Morrison

The station at Welham Green (south of Hatfield) was opened to passengers in September 1986, and provides fairly basic facilities. Class 31 No. 31451 is seen passing on the down fast line with a ballast train on Sunday 10th January 1988.

On the same day, Class 47 No. 47610 heads the Overhead Line Maintenance Train, working on the down slow line south of Brookmans Park.

North from Cricklewood

Above: Class 45 No. 45150 (unofficially named *Vampire*) hauls a Cricklewood to Cliffe Hill ballast train, north of Hendon on 18th September 1987.

Left: Another train to originate from Cricklewood is the twice-daily "Binliner" destined for Forders Sidings on the Bedford to Bletchley line. Class 45 No. 45033 is seen on this working, north of Luton, in May 1986.

London Nightlife

A fascinating variety of evening departures can be witnessed at the various London termini including sleeper, motorail, and Post Office traffic. On Saturday evenings in early 1988, no less than eight trains conveying newspapers left Paddington in a four-hour period, including 1C03, the 00.50 to Bristol Temple Meads, which was headed by Class 50 No. 50022 *Anson* on 23rd January 1988. Newspaper traffic ceased some six months later.

On one of its last visits to London, Class 50 No. 50011 *Centurion* awaits departure time with the 22.25 Penzance postal train, at Paddington, on 4th February 1987. Later the same month, *Centurion* became the first "Hoover" to be withdrawn from service.

Deputising for the diagrammed Class 50 locomotive, Class 37 No. 37096, of Tinsley TMD, has charge of 4B71, the 21.50 Paddington to Gloucester vans, on 2nd January 1988.

The familiar sight and sound of 'Deltics' at King's Cross disappeared at the end of 1981 after more than twenty years of service, but these much-admired machines will always be associated with the London terminus of the East Coast Main Line. Only a few weeks before the end, No. 55008 *The Green Howards* awaits departure with the 22.15 to Aberdeen, which travelled over 400 miles before the first advertised stop, at Inverkeithing.

At the other end of Platform 1, No. 55004 *Queen's Own Highlander* is seen after arrival with the 15.50 semi-fast from York, on 10th February 1980.
Graham Wood

Bereft of headcode discs, Class 40 No. 40058 waits to work the lightweight 22.45 King's Cross to Newcastle newspaper train (1N08) on 20th June 1984.

Another newspaper train, but from the adjacent St Pancras terminus, was entrusted to Class 40 haulage on Saturday night 8th September 1984, when No. 40122 took charge of 1P01, the 00.20 to Derby, returning north after railtour duty. Several enthusiasts can be seen on the platform hopeful of a look round the cab of the green-liveried celebrity locomotive, before departure. On the right, Class 317 emu No. 317345 forms the 00.45 train to Bedford.

Euston station normally sees only electric traction on passenger trains, but occasionally the removal of the overhead power supply to facilitate engineering work leads to the use of diesel power. On 8th January 1989, a three-car Class 117 unit was photographed prior to departure as the 00.26 service to Milton Keynes.

The second generation of diesel multiple units have yet to make an impact on passenger services in the London area. However, prototype Sprinter units Nos 150001 and 151001 made a number of non-stop trial runs between Derby and St Pancras in 1985, and were photographed prior to the return journey down the Midland Main Line on 5th October that year.

Ken Brunt

The loss of newspaper traffic in July 1988, deprived the enthusiast of much of noturnal interest at the London termini. Two departures from Paddington which can no longer be seen are depicted here. The 23.35 to Westbury (Passenger and News) was entrusted to Class 50 No. 50025 *Invincible* on the misty evening of 16th January 1988, (above), whilst on Saturday 9th July, the final departure of the 22.10 (Newspapers) to Milford Haven (below) was powered by Class 47 No. 47417.